Praise for
This Going, This Grace
by Maureen Sweeney Ackerman

"As Maureen Ackerman writes in a characteristically tough and tender poem, 'Everything sings for love.' Her poems arise like a soloist in a choir, whose individual beauty and brilliance occur within and depend on her awareness of the group. She is of and for this world, yet perched above it, too, involved in what she calls 'the trick of stars.' Here is a dazzling poet. Here is a lyrical, generous heart."

—Roger Rosenblatt, author of *Making Toast* and *Kayak Morning*

"Maureen Ackerman's poems are fresh and ardent and ravishing. Her images—a bird poised on the lip of a pool; a deer captured in the chapel of dusk—come from a simple world, the natural world, yet she transforms them into symbols of radiance, of transcendence. Ackerman writes from a place of true understanding: of the knotty complexity of love, the inexorability of time, the enduring consolations of nature. Her poems have depth and reach but also an unmistakable lightness. They are infused by something she writes about often: grace."

—Jessica Teich, author of the memoir *The Future Tense of Joy*

"Maureen Ackerman writes from the deepest part of her heart about her experiences witnessing the miracles of nature. There is a spiritual quality of a higher power that flows from her writing. I recommend this book as a must read for people who love nature but may have trouble finding the words to share their feelings with others."

— Gerald G. Jampolsky, M.D., author of *Love is Letting Go of Fear*

"The thing I love the most about Maureen Ackerman's poems is how they're never in a hurry. They move carefully, intellectually, and emotionally to their conclusion, and in doing so we are witnesses to the complications of the mind and how it addresses topics like love and loss, and so much more. The poems beautifully contain these movements within the stuff of the world—leaves, crows, blood, the brain, the sky. Her images are often haunting. Yet her choice of musical phrases is both deft and comforting. Her poetry is just plain lovely."

> — Michael Henry, author of *No Stranger Than My Own*
> and *Active Gods*

"Maureen Ackerman's poems are filled with deep love and wisdom. They take you on wild journeys of reflection and immersion into sublime beauty, lift you up in ecstatic surrender, and then hold you very close to the warm light of the soul of this world, with so much tenderness that you will, indeed, find light streaming everywhere, from you. What a gift she embodies, and what a gift for the reader to be invited into her world!"

> — Sergio Baroni, LCSW, Psychotherapist,
> contributing author in *Ready, Set, Live!*

"In lyrical language, Maureen Ackerman's poems express the beauty and transcendence of life and love. They are infused with both the hard grace of loving what is difficult and the tenderness of living through the light. I feel blessed and inspired by reading *This Going, This Grace.*"

> — Marci Shimoff, #1 NY Times bestselling author,
> *Happy for No Reason* and *Chicken Soup for the Woman's Soul*

THIS GOING, THIS GRACE

This Going, This Grace

Poems

Maureen Sweeney Ackerman

GROK PRESS
Denver, Colorado

Book design by Mariah Parker mettagraphics.com
Cover photo by Daniel Ackerman

ISBN 978-1-7337175-2-6
Library of Congress Control Number: 2019941524

Grok Press
www.grokpress.net
maureen@grokpress.net

ACKNOWLEDGMENTS

Thanks to the following people, without whom these poems would have remained scribblings on scattered pages:

Gary Ackerman and Danny Ackerman, who are unwavering in their love and support.

Karen Cirincione, who has envisioned this book for years, patiently editing and guiding it toward publication.

Mariah Parker, who creatively embraced the task of long-distance design.

Jeff Shusterman, who listens and believes in what I do.

Bobby Sullivan, who reads like a writer and offers the honest, detailed feedback a writer needs.

I love not Man the less, but Nature more.

— Lord Byron

CONTENTS

Preface

An image: My father, head bent to a book, at home among page people in a world made up out of words. An idea: That I could enter that world, that I could count on its constancy, imagine its truth. Little wonder, then, that I'd make a life out of what I loved: Words, and their power to make things—to make us—known and knowable.

And why not? Growing up in a place called Poet's Corner, in the shadow of a church and school and convent named for St. Brigid, patron saint of poets and sweet saint of compassion, what was an Irish girl to do with all that stained glass suffering and someday-salvation and insistence on what couldn't be seen? Gather it, of course; translate it; practice forever *how to keep a quiet eye, how to hear the seed becoming, how to be the child bent sideways to the light.* On the north shore of Long Island, where I later lived on Convent Drive and watched the sea and sky stretch in impossible light, the girl grew old, but the eye still looked toward what the heart might hear, and the pen skipped faithfully across the page.

Now that *I've gathered up the simple stems and petals that the years have rearranged*, I realize more clearly than ever the connection between our sense of place and our sense of self. My mother was right: *Everything* (and every place) *has something it can tell.*

— Maureen Sweeney Ackerman
April 2019
Denver, Colorado

THIS GOING, THIS GRACE

I

*I love that in the landscape of my own mind,
I can begin again…*

LOVE ENOUGH

I love the verb *to be*,
that it all comes down to
I am, I have been, I shall be.
And the most active verb of all,
to love,
that the present tense is the same for all of us:
I love, you love.
That love is the best subject of all,
that we all want to be its object.

I love that creation comes through love,
that eyes, nose, mouth
reshape into how we know each other,
and that we show ourselves
before we see ourselves,
that we begin with an act of faith:
We get seen.

I love how we discover our bodies,
how even in the dark
we can be found, we can feel who we are.
That we learn about separation
through fingers, toes,
that they pull and spread apart
and stay connected:
We're never not bound to ourselves.
I love that we can move away,
then come back.

I love the acts of movement,
how day lights into itself,
how light plays games

with the ground
and wins, life issuing
on light's terms.
I love that light forgives,
that we are light, forgiven.

And I love that forgiveness
belongs to us, that we can let go
of how we hurt,
that it can happen anywhere,
not just inside a church,
although a church will have a way.
I love the cold, kind joy in statues,
the dependable half-smiles,
the eyes transfixed,
before or after absolution they're the same.
I love stained glass, suffering
sun-washed and sprayed
in rainbow arcs.
I love Latin prayers,
the wisdom of what we won't know,
sometimes.

And I love how we learn to know.
About longing, for instance,
the pull of what's outside the frame, endless.
How water flirts and woos us
so we think we can be held
and float along, an easy going.
I love how we let ourselves be lulled,
a little.

And leaving, too, the western sky,
sun-striped and defiant before it dies,
life losing itself in declaration.
I love that both have a sense of time,
that they sense when they're in sync,
then let go, get out of each other's way.
A believing by balance.

And how good to go off balance, caught
by a careless crossing of ducklings
where always are cars.
I love the circuitous route,
the side street that surprises
when you wind up at water
and don't want to back up,
the road that goes
out of its way to get you lost.

And how not to love being lost,
in the fertile field of your own
sweet dream, the bloom
now become a bouquet.
I love gardens,
wild ones especially, resourceful
enough to find a way back,
to flower without you.
I love their honesty, that they're beautiful
without any work.

And work, too, with its own beauty,
hands that make things,

minds that decide, decipher.
I love working my body, running
until I'm somewhere else,
at the beach, maybe,
the Connecticut coastline a constant.
A back road somewhere,
honeysuckle sweet in summer,
nobody else around.
I love a slightly wet world in morning,
leaves still shiny with last night's rain,
the clean smell of what's beginning.

I love that in the landscape of my own mind,
I can begin again, there,
a new line,
new arrangement of words,
new sentence that startles
when the worn out idea starts over.

And I love that over and over,
we start over,
that we stay in endless cycle,
am, was, shall be.
And that the cycle,
the circle of everyone
and everything that lives,
is love enough.

I I

I thought about the way things find their grace...

WHERE IT STARTS

Go watch the grass grow, my mother used to say
those summers long ago,
when afternoons were wider than imagination
and I was underfoot, no school or lists that needed
    checking off.
And listen, she'd add, her voice a whisper-tickle to my ear.
Everything has something it can tell.

Off I'd set to measure green through empty minutes
the way my mother measured me through early years.
Ten minutes, forty, a week: What difference did it make
that I lay alert for some tilt upward,
some shiver or spurt that I could count as the day's worth,
some secret I could barter for attention's sake.

No matter. The grass in its own pulse would have none
    of me
and my hungry watch, and I would have nothing
to report come dinner time. But through the too-few years
she'd yet to live, Mother never asked what it was I found
as day after day I looked out and around and down
at a world not bound by words,

as little by little I learned those lessons
best when left unsaid:

how to keep a quiet eye,
how to hear the seed becoming,
how to be the child bent sideways to the light.

MOTHER'S DAY

She sees them from inside first, lilacs
she had missed from the other side,
and needing so the moment's clearer view,
she rubs at winter grit until the glass
is all but gone and she is looking through
to faraway, where every May
her mother sang a hymn of lilac praise
and brushed a branch of blooms along their skin
till they became a sweetness of their own,
a fragrance held as first discovered love.

Lilacs, her mother sang.
I will love you like lilacs forever.

Here near the sea, the trees are blooming still,
insistent as her mother's eyes on her,
as if blossoms were a way of bending sight,
as if the dead might see her bending now
to coax the fold lines from the faded sheet
that years ago had soothed her mother's skin,
its cares and fretting shed in chemo sheets
till it was white-blue new,
while the sour stench of cancer filled the bed,
the room, her tired lungs,

and lilacs filled the fresh spring yard beyond
against the dimming light inside.

At St. John's Pond

This morning a swan
      set across St. John's Pond
           like a thing slipping into love,

like a ballet bride trailing a netty veil.
      From where I sat
           on a mossy space of stone,

I could not see
      what waited on the other side,
           what moved the reeds and grasses

like some shiver of wind on harp-string,
      some finger of praise, lifting.
           But watching her easy slide

to the silky shore, I imagined
      this must be how life begins,
           how it spills into itself:

a white light gliding,
      a quick glimmer of ecstasy,
           the clear blue center of day.

With a Different Lens

I might have imagined it, the robin
poised on the lip of the pool like a swimmer
leaning toward a lap.
I could have been dreaming
the sparrows and chickadees, come
to slap the water in arcs of applause.
But standing on the other side
of back door glass, I knew I was seeing
what would have happened without me:
the world going on.

On an afternoon warm past winter,
birds paused for a while in a backyard pool,
they whirled and wet their wings
with last night's rain,
and then were gone, singing.
I might have wished them stay,
or take me with them,
but they were birds,
they were not here for holding.

Watching them fly off, relaxed
and shimmery, I thought about
the way things find their grace:

birds on some slip of air,
we meant for earth, inventing

some wing of fancy,
some trick of faith,
some way to hold on.

SAINT SKY

When I needed to, I'd make him up,
    a beautiful breeze of boy I believed
        into being, my saint of air and sky.

Closing my eyes, I would call
    and he'd float through, all foggy mist,
        lifting us up till we'd land light

as lint on some ruffle of leaf.
    We would lie there, close
        to the center, listening

to what stirred underneath, a language
    he said was all splash and color
        and wind-magnet, while we learned

how to wait for one
    glorious gust to sweep us
        loose, sail us in swishy loops

over park and puddle and woodpath,
    till we tumbleswayed home,
        two earth things formed new

through flight. Leaving,
    he would thank me, his whisperkiss
        the only prayer I knew, and fade away.

Now steamy space,
    now sky,
        now air.

And I'd breathe.

Something Like Prayer

For weeks I had been thinking about prayer,
the easy way that words became forgiveness

on Saturday afternoons at the old stone church,
when the priest would wave away your weekly sins

and float his absolution through the dark
till you were lifting light like some songbird

in praise, or like a poem you form from pain,
from polishing your sorrow till it shines.

Last night a deer walked out beyond the woods,
it stepped across the shadows and it stood,

a statue in a chapel made of dusk.
Oh, it had a mouth, it had a tongue,

some alphabet of sound it might have made.
But it held to air, it held hard to my eyes,

it held there quiet, still as stepping stones.
And then it turned, and lifting toward the hill,

it spoke in wordless syllables of grace,
in couplets like some wild and perfect prayer.

E-Mail Note to a Young Writer

Everyone was going on about the Millennium,
one century turning into the next,
but I had nothing to contribute about a sudden epiphany
as the world wondered, or celebrated,
what movement means. I knew only that on January 1,

the sky stretched in loose folds across Long Island Sound
as it had been stretching day after day,
and isn't the ordinariness of it all what is really
    remarkable,
that the sea flows on as the sky cradles clouds
without ever turning a calendar page?

And now I tell it to you, I give you what I see
to know as your own, and to know me,
which is what mankind has been doing forever
in symbol or sound or letter, wanting to be known,
but I do it in this twenty-first century e-mail,

which is an instant thing and a keepable grace,
for I have recorded myself, too, what I have noticed.
Yesterday turned from winter freeze to warming,
and ducks played in a puddle of melted ice,
and I thought about you, about what you called

melting the freeze of the heart,
and I send you this note to read as a young writer
turning toward love that lets him see
everything through a brightened eye,
infusing the world with a kindness

that comes back and back.
Notice the pond at the church, the curve
wrapping like tenderness around the swans.
Watch the little tree bloom into itself, and
look how stars punctuate the sky in exclamation.

Everything is for you. Everything sings for love.

BIRTHDAY
for Karen and Sandra

March,
and moonlight touches trees
like a mother tracing
the delicate length of body
new in her arms.
Branches bend against night,
and wind sighs into song,
a hundred notes of happiness
curling across the sky,
singing you into a self.

SCOTT'S BEACH

Up here the cold waits like a priest,
it opens its fingers toward you,
it sings its *alleluia* through the woods,
its *peace be with you*,
and you run your response
into the trails, into the snow,
you shape the syllables with your feet:
and also with you.

Along the hills and dips
your body pumps, it pours itself
into the day, into the absolution
of icy air and you are clean,
you take the snow like a wafer
to your tongue,
you let it melt, let it drip,
you swallow

until you are hot inside,
until you are filled with the white
fire of redemption,
until you are a breathy mist lifting
like morning, like Eve
forming from Adam,
rising out of his rib
into her own.

Mother to Son, at Twenty-One

There are things a mother's heart should know:
the way her child can greet the day,
open, willing partner to the light
of what life means, hope
and faith that good will grow
in shades of gentle things.

And other things,
too, she'll want to know:
how her own longings grow,
root themselves in how she welcomes day,
then gather hope
and in her child, light

a way to fullness, light
to carry, dreams of things
made whole by lasting hope.
A mother wants to know
through dry, cracked day
that seeds she plants still grow,

fed by her child's hunger, grow
toward their own light
to find in greener day
visions of self, allowing things
to pass through her, knowing
that her hope

makes memory, shapes his life with hope
and grace, growing
wonder, washing over what he knows

to help him lighten
fears, invent the things
by which he'll claim his day.

And now, your life has flowered toward this day,
it celebrates the blossom of old hope
and holds the blessed center of all things,
your heart, that in its simple sweetness grows
in ever-grateful light
as your reaching arms proclaim, *I am. I know.*

So sing out, Son, your birthday song a thing
of lasting light. Your mother's heart
knows hope in how you grow.

III

*...in the ragged ache of loss there hung the question
how to hold or go, let go...*

THIS GOING, THIS GRACE

When the stories had been told and retold,
when the poems and prayers had been spoken
and there was nothing else to say
for Arthur Frame except Amen, the Pastor said

for the living, "Let the heavens guide,"
so tonight we've shut the lights,
tonight we turn to stars and the swollen moon
to glow inside the old gray shingled house

where I watch with Anne, whose Arthur
last week scattered breakfast toast
on frozen snow between backyard shrubs
and the seaside bluff so gulls might swoop,

or even crows, which were, of course,
just being crows—*They need to do
the thing they do*—and then Arthur
did a thing Anne could not stop,

which was to stop mid-sentence:
*Why, look now, Anne, there's a kind of beauty
in the shine of those black wings, and is that—*
And that was it. She had been trying to see

what he meant about beauty, crows against snow
like ink on a linen page,
she had been trying to find a familiar turn
in the foreign language of their scrawl—

See, a little thank you they're scratching—
so when Arthur dropped to the floor beside her feet,

light as any bird on a barren slope, she was sure
it was for crumbs he'd left behind—*Got to feed*

the hungry now, let's not forget the hungry—
and watching so the birds beyond the glass
beyond her reach, Anne never saw her Arthur
slip beyond the reach of all they'd known

of almost fifty years, she did not notice
breath and sigh gone still until he'd gone
for good, her Arthur, who had fed the birds
and his wife's heart in faithful measure.

Years ago, my mother limped
a slow, hard trek toward death,
the breakdown lung by bone by brain,
and one October seasons later, my sister died,

quick as the pull of spent leaves from their branch,
and in the ragged ache of loss there hung the question
how to live the dying, and the death,
how to hold or go, let go, with grace.

Now Anne holds the needle
of remembered years
against the vein of love that is her heart,
but she's afraid, she says, afraid of memory,

afraid of this bristling moment
and the gleaming, unspeakable next,
afraid of the black bird
and the shimmering tease of the wing,

afraid of all the knowing
and the not knowing at all,
until from a clearing beyond the fear
comes the poet's call to keep the questions close,

as if the questions could finally save your life,
as if the inscrutable eye of the moon and the trick of stars
were finally questions cast as gratitude,
or grief.

Daughters of Wisdom, All

Always

People should die on Fridays, my mother says
when there is nothing else she can say
about the dead. People should die on Fridays,
in the rain.

1953

June, a parking lot beneath a second-floor window,
a hospital, my mother next to me, pointing up.
Peggy, my aunt whose hair is red
like the sky toward night,
she is there behind the window bars,
but there is no sky, there is a face under a cap,
and then another face, tiny, another hat.
My mother says, Colleen,
and I am looking for curls,
for hair the color of corn.
I am looking for my cousin, three and sick.

July, the cemetery, we live
three houses down from the fence.
In a certain light, in a certain season,
we see new graves.
My mother is at the edge of the lawn,
she is leaning out, twisting
her head, watching. My mother is crying.

Angel of God, my guardian dear.

1956

My mother and I along the cemetery road
past the train station, toward church,
toward the Stations of the Cross.
The sky is gray like the cemetery gates,
and we are cold, we try to keep under the umbrella.
It is Good Friday.
It is raining, it is raining more.
Remember, my mother tells me.

In memory of me.

1978

Another hospital, named for a saint,
the Daughters of Wisdom at work.
It is Friday, September 1,
the sky blue like veins
between earth and heaven,
the sun like a watchful eye.
I am the mother of a son,
my mother dies,
and in the chapel, I kneel in the dark,
and I wonder
where is the rain.

2000

Moving, life ever moving.

The movers strip the rooms,
the movers store the years, and living.

I run to the new land,
I run to the holy, hallowed land,
the convent grounds, the consecrated ground,
where the Daughters of Wisdom say my name.

Blessed are the merciful. Blessed, blessed.

The day thick with heat,
the day thick with haze,
high above Long Island Sound,
the water still, birds insisting on song,
shouting their praise,
fluttering their prayer.

We are in the world to love the world,
love and love.

It is Friday, September 1.

2005

Story has it that they came to the shore
before passing, these nuns,
Sisters to the sick, Daughters of Wisdom,
that they danced to the beach
and disappeared.
Oh, look! This is the sway of light,
a slight skip across sand, a slide into the sea,
a slipping of skin, a lifting up, an offering:

This is my body.

And a spin, a spiral into sky.

Always

Oh, easy the shedding of skin!
Oh, light the wing!
My mother lifting among them,
wisdom's women all,
these weightless shapes across the day,
these blessings of belief,
these brave waves of hope.

WHAT KEEPS

It's digging does the heart its earthly good,
she used to say, and kneeling to the soil
as if it were communion that she sought,
and kindly light,
she'd reach her fingers far into the ground
until at last she touched
some perfect place for roots,
for teaching us the properties of earth,
the beauty in what's tangled underneath.

Seasons later, her body and her breath,
her longings, stilled, I wondered
how we'd lay her in the ground,
how we'd dig a grief hole kind enough and deep
to hold the flesh that held her innerness
and let it drift like grace notes on the day.

Today her grandson crawled beyond the shade
and shadows of the leafy arms of oaks,
and in a motion loose as her last breath,
he lifted like some flower toward the sun
and moved his legs like stems in subtle breeze.
The music in the air was not from wind
but from some wild and grateful ache of love,
and through the skin of grass around her grave,
the singing that her bones made underneath.

Why Winter

January, and the cold deepens,
snow slides from the dull sky
through moonless nights
across the fields,
onto the roofs and yards,
into the woods,
and still the thermometer dips,
wind pushes over the sea
and under the sea

into swell after swell
against the sand,
against the bulkhead,
wind against the porch,
against the doors,
insistent as memory,
then finally a thin blue light
on the skeleton frames of trees,
stiff and rigid as the now frozen sea.

Yesterday I sat beside the bed of my father,
frozen inside Parkinson's
and the bony frame of a half-life,
his memory and mine twisted
like the sad bend of fingers
that cannot unclamp,
nails that dig into skin
until it bleeds a way toward redemption,
an *Our Father* of the flesh.

Tell me about love, I said,
how a father might love
a daughter finally,

and because words could not come
from his tired tongue,
I told him about loving my son,
I spoke a poem about hope in how a child grows,
and I saw in the blank eyes of my father
what might have passed for tears.

Here is the argument for winter,
the hard grace of loving what is difficult,
of crawling into the dark cave of the heart,
and emerging in a stubborn glimmer of light.

So You Know
for Gael Blair

When Colleen called to tell me you had died,
I listened like a nerve, exposed.

I looked at the sky, certain I would find it
black and empty, but the stars were there
in little families, they went on being stars,
and the moon was lighting treetops
as though nothing had changed in the night.

I touched the autumn flowers in the basket,
I told them you had left, told them
Gael, she's gone,
and still their petals softened in my fingers,
still they spilled their scent into my hands.

Holly leaves were holding up red berries,
and Long Island sounded like itself,
crickets calling to each other
things that crickets need to know.
Next day I ran to the beach,

and when I told it *Gael,*
when I said *Gael* to the skin of water
on the sand, it took your name, trickled
it back into its throat and swallowed,
then drew away.

But the wave came back, it touched easy
to the shore, and I took it to me,
I cupped and washed it over me
as if to mix it in me like
some pin-prick of blood, some promise

that a sister should have made.
Grief needed to breathe.
Today October falls in furious light,
it falls from maples and oaks,
it flames itself onto the day.

Leaves rip from branches here, they twist
like flecks of memory through the air,
while trees curve and bend away,
content to do what trees do:
Let go what they have spent a season loving.

Under my feet, the leaves are settling in.
They know you are coming.

SOMETHING OF A FACT
for Dr. Jim Lynch

Because he knows about the body,
he is a realist, he says.
Doctors. So many facts to face.
So much to know.

But the history of the body, I say,
it's the history of the heart,
scars of skin and spirit
stitched into who we are.
The doctor,
he's like the priest,
pulling miracles from the fact of our frailty,
blessing us whole.

Facts:
He helped us to breathe, to walk again,
to open our ears, to patch our wounds,
and ourselves.

What is the word for salvation?
Do you call that love?

Summer, years ago,
we are on the porch,
we are talking about my father,
who has died.
Your father loved you, he says.
He nods toward the hydrangeas
blooming around us. Irish eyes,
he says about the blue.
It's who we are.

A fact of weather:
For weeks it had rained,
dark days turned to darker nights,
then finally a Thursday morning,
blue and clean
and singing,
sun so strong you could not look
straight on at so much light.

You had to close your eyes,
you had to open yourself,
you had to shine
from the sweetness inside.

How do you answer?
Do you call that faith?

Today the sky emptied again,
hail like stones of sadness
against the porch,
the blue hydrangeas bending
toward the ground,
then quiet,
and an explosion of light.

Did you see it, the rainbow,
bending from there to here?
Is that called an arc of hope?

This is not about sorrow,
though surely we can say how that feels.
This is about living through the light,
about knowing who we are.

I V

*Today I've gathered up the simple stems
and petals that the years have rearranged...*

A NEAR OCCASION

Tuesday, 10 o'clock. They are driving toward water.
He has called his hunger breakfast. What he wants
   is more.
He is not thinking about the woman who wakes him
   into day,
who waits through the half-light of later,
measures what a marriage ever means.
He is thinking about the woman in his car,
that he is falling in love.

What he wants is this: excavation.
He wants her to discover him,
dig deep where he is dead, buried in the living
room of home, to reach the still life
of his self, motionless as a body years in bed.
He wants her as air, as breeze that can stir him.

The radio is playing. She is singing along:
Never been lied to, never denied.
He believes that she means this.

She has seen his sadness,
the shape of how he hurts.
She understands in her woman's heart
what he is wanting.
She knows about needs,
the desperate hope inside them.
She wonders about her own,
how she has let herself into his loneliness.
She decides to notice morning,
trees along turning roads,
sun on sidewalks.

She hears a voice inside her head,
twists the ring that roots her.

He is trying to tell her something.
Flowers are good, he says,
and water, too, and children.
Later, when he smells summer at the harbor,
he tells her, boats. And August heat.

I like in-between, she says, and wonders
if it's weather that she's meaning,
June still April sometimes, May in March.
It's movement, she's thinking,
a floating kind of fancy, in and out.
It's fiction, inventing what's real.

He is pointing out: Boston Whaler.
I grew up on a Boston Whaler.
And she sees him ten, twelve, twenty,
lost boy come to drift a way toward home.

Water is movement, too, she wants to tell him,
another way of being in-between.
It's all longing and leaving
and never really landing, locking in.
It's a loose-fit loving.
Lets you go light.

He has been looking at her.
She lets him look, long.

What happens next is waiting
to be invented.

She says this: Let's go.
It is enough to know
that they are choosing.
It's part of what passes,
part of what never gets named.

Anniversary Poem

Last night, all night, the snow came,
it came in strands, it came in ribbons,
until it half-became a quilt
like the one we found in Nantucket,
in the shop past the cobblestone courtyard,
where pink and purple and white—
purple, mostly, deep, like day about to darken—
spilled from copper containers into the breeze
until the petals looked like birds in party dress,
fluttering across the astonished air.

Cosmos, the flower girl told us,
and you laughed, you said, of course,
the world in a wildflower,
and we carried some back to the room,
and all night we made the world
out of bone and skin,
out of silky ribbons for sky
and the blessed geography of a bed beneath us,
an ocean to dive and drown until sun washed
through window lace and we surfaced,
lovesplashed,

like this morning's pine beyond the window,
a bride splashed snowy from last night's love,
from the heave of sky spilling desire
to his sleepy dream below,
until she opened her arms,
until she opened herself,
to the longing loose in the swirls.

Marry me, he sang, *marry me,*
and through the startled silence
her body quivered with the happy cry,
the grateful gasp, *I do.*
Oh, I do.

TRANSLATION

When you cannot love with the body,
you can love with words, he said,
and she said she would adore him while he read
and he agreed he would adore her listening
and she thought that it would matter what he chose
though she could not at first say why

it was the story of the woman drowning,
sinking in the swollen sea
while her father stood and stared,
but not at her, not at the mouth
without sound, not at the eyes speaking
sadness thick as a rope that cannot pull
her in unless he throws it,
unless he forgets the men
who dragged him kicking from the sea,
who spoke into his unblinking eyes about bodies,
bodies, so many bodies swimming
over him, around him, calling his name
like the young priest behind the altar
to look, look at the key, how it slips
into the hole of the gold tabernacle
that holds the white ring
that means redemption,
but he would not wear the ring,
he will not twist the rope into a ring
for his daughter to wear,
he will not watch his daughter sink at last
into the hold of the man who is there
watching for his own salvation,
he will not see the man's words
float like a tender string toward her,
until hand over hand she finds it,

she pulls herself toward him,
and they touch,
they touch everywhere,
and they know what it is
to be saved by so true a thing.

So he put the book down.
So he moved toward her.
Life happens in the body, he said,
and they spoke and they spoke
in the radiant language of skin.

On Grace Bay

Late afternoons from the porch I watch

how the turquoise is so light it shimmers, all swell
    and spray
and the sun moves toward it, a slow slipping
    and lowering
and it hangs for a moment on the edge
of where the sea will open and receive it
and the sun is full of fire and burning
until this impossible blue sucks it in, swallows it
and what has pulsed and longed is lost in foamy relief
inside the wet expansive secret of what's beneath

and it will move again in morning away, away
it will mount, it will climb high, so high
it sees all of what it loves below
and this blue will shimmer still
and the sun will swell with heat
and long again toward the sea
toward where the sea is deep and waiting

and the sun will rise and fall
and it will rise and fall more
and it will vibrate over and over
toward its own dying
so it can come again into life
because it will never have enough

and I call it this:
how I know you.

In the Language of Leaves

Oh, look how morning stretches wide and high
around us while the faithful leaves begin
to brush against the ever open sky
like fingers touching onto willing skin.

And look how later, when the ease of blue
is lost inside the ache of grayer air,
the leaves keep reaching out the way you do
to soothe this heart's concern and body's wear.

If I possessed the language of the leaves,
the eloquence of late October flame,
I'd have my heart recite what it receives
in syllables that celebrate your name.

But let the leaves speak for me, and you'll know:
My love is there, disguised as autumn glow.

Skin, Listening

She imagines it this way,
her head in the drum
that he's slamming,
her hands holding air.
It is mid-time, sometime,
no sun, no space, no sky.
She sees only skin,
skin from the inside,
white like milk, stretched smooth.
They are moving, she thinks,
metal against stone, hard.
Her bones are what he bangs with,
she is left without form,
she forgets how to feel.

Later she sees it this way,
her skin a soft sheet.
He dances her high now,
they are smooth against smooth,
slide against slide,
they are fire, a full
quick explosion.

And a hush.

They have made of themselves
sweet starry sky.

HAPPINESS

I picked some flowers earlier today
and later watched you settle on the porch
to read your magazine in easy peace
and rock some through this lazy August heat
in the old wood chair that knows a season's needs.

The little table, yellow as the sun
we used to seek, stood next to where you sat,
and in the corner, in the antique glass
as blue and clear as sea, or afternoon,
were daisies that I'd placed with all the love
that on another August afternoon
I spoke inside the small white harbor church,
where the air was filled with daisies spilling love
in seeds of stubborn hope I'd learn to sow.

Today I've gathered up the simple stems
and petals that the years have rearranged.
I bring you the bouquet that they've become:
this happiness of bone and skin and vein.

CHRISTMAS EVE

How it must matter

that we're alive in love's sight,
that we're holding love's light,
that I'm writing these words
for you on this night,
that you're holding these words
as you hold me, in light,
and sacred love, this silent night.

V

All we need to know, said the poet, is beauty...

Like Lazarus
for Dr. Mark Wasserman

You lean toward the folder,
history in your hand, the present
in search of a script.
You study the litany
of broken bones,
an eye without a retina,
an empty womb.
And pneumonia.

August, years ago,
I am slumped
in a hospital bed,
I am here and not here,
I am floating to the women
who float in their oceany robes.
I am trying to shine, I am trying
to see through the light
of so much love. I cannot
unclose my eyes. I cannot
open my mouth,
or myself.

You are suddenly there, you
open your hand, you
touch me to your side.
I am Lazarus,
summoned to life
by the swell of kindness,
by the alchemy of love,

until the day of diminishing
when I do not know I am Lazarus,
when the name for sun is not friend
and for mass is not prayer
and the only name I know
is *yes,* all things *yes,*
even you, you are *yes,*
there again, bedside, whispering,
saying the unsayable,
this thing called

Cancer,
crasher at the brain gate,
word thief, dream thief,
sower of instability,
until now, months later,
I know the names of things, doctor
things you will add to the litany:

meningioma
melanoma
glioblastoma

and, yes, I know I am Lazarus,
again I am Lazarus, alive.

Maybe *yes* is everything, I say,
as you study me
and the folder of the past.
Now add the present tense, I say,
and the future tense,
the shape of all days,
the shape of this heart.

Please write that I name it
gratitude.

Please write that I say
your name.

What Comes Next

This is about her dying, her being dead,
about what happens to the body
when the breathing stops.
Gael's dying, Gael's body.
Gael, born in March when the winds wouldn't quit,
named in their honor to live in their dangerous thrill.
Terrible. Beautiful. Fierce and ferocious and wild.

Your mother, her son remembers, *come quick.*
Oh, how can quick translate to traffic,
to freeways on a Monday afternoon?
What can quick mean
when it's your mother the hospital is holding,
when your mother is Gael,
who is storm,
who is March,
who is fifty years' wind without cease?

Do you know?

Afternoon in October, anonymous, ordinary.
Gael dies, disappears,
she floats into air with the leaves,
spinning away.
She dies without words,
without language for dying,
but she speaks with her arms to her son.
She leans, she longs,
and because he needs to,
because he is her first born,
he listens to the longing,
he makes it the last sound he hears,
a hymn to forever.

The living, they have ritual.
But what is the ritual of the wind died down?

Do you know?

Boxing her body, oh, cruel, cruel,
containing the wind.
Be kind, be kind. Scatter her,
disperse her like a blessing.

But her father has a grave, he has buried his wife,
and he will bury his daughter, too.

February, her father says: They have the body. I have
    the grave.
He says: My daughter, my daughter, give my first-born girl
    a grave.
Her son says: My mother, my mother, let my mother loose.
Her daughter says: I don't know, I don't know.

Now they say nothing.
Silence, sad like a deep, dark sin.
A hole, a hurt in the heart.

Now her ashes sit on a shelf,
they wait in a box,
they wait for burial
next to her mother.
The silence waits, too,
it hangs like a leaf in delicate poise,
waiting for the wind to claim it,
to send it where dead leaves go.

OBIT, UPDATE

"I am your own way of looking at things," she said.
And I took her hand. —William Stafford

Today gulls loop across afternoon like exclamation,
the glimmery lift of the heart in a promise kept.
Goldenrod bends from the bluff like bodies in praise,
and clouds ruffle white along the horizon,
soft, the shape of salvation.

It is Friday, the first of September,
and though I had meant to write
about the day she died,
Friday, the first of September,
though this was to be a reminder about death,

about the world stabbed cold that day,
the sun all needles of light from the veiny sky,
these late summer leaves are scattering like kisses,
fingers of beachgrass tremble toward their touch,
and Listen! the gullwings, a love song, the flutter of
    the heart.

So I tell you about living, about how she is here.

HYMN FOR FRANCIE BLISS

At Shining Shores, where nothing gleams and puddles pass
    for sea,
it's Sunday, and the priest prays for the frail,
who hang and bow like birds before St. Francis in cement,
the statue that the failing call Big F before they beg
    for shine themselves.
Can you be instruments of peace? the Father asks,

but Francie Bliss says peace is wings, wings
that she's been stitching from the feathers she can
    feel, wings
that flap her to the shore nobody sees, wings
that flutter through the birdbath of the blue
until she sheds her skin for good, oh, she has shed a thing
    or two,

she shed pajamas for a man who kissed her parts
    and ripped
her womanhood and flew for good himself, *Ha, Ha,*
    she cries.
Nobody says a thing, but Father sings, *Salvation if*
    you see,
Amen, Amen. And Francie Bliss waves like a light from
    the wild
as she falls into flight.

How We Might Imagine It
for Patricia Walsh McKay

What I am telling you is true:
Winter melted down, and finally
Long Island Sound unfroze, the swan
that had swum the length of shore returned,
it was there on the sea like a white silk sash
on the delicate shoulder of blue afternoon.
Blue, like an eye opening in long-ago June.
Blue, like a wide-brimmed hat framing the clear
and open dazzle of a woman's face.
Blue, like a dress for celebration,
or a body bent in the shape of grief.

Oh, what can a swan know of its own beauty,
or a woman hers? What can we ever know?

All we need to know, said the poet, is beauty,
which is also truth, which is, I think, a glimmer
of eternity from this bone-house
of the body where we live.

The day after I learned our Patsy died,
I found on the sand outside my house
the slumped and lifeless body of the swan,
its face framed by a ruffle of wings in rest.
Maybe Shelley was right.
Maybe we need to imagine what we know.
And maybe the swan, and Patsy, imagined
the curious voice of God singing them on,
and they imagined a mercy the living need.

In late summer, a daughter returned one final time
to the family that had watched her laugh and shine.

Then she rode a train to Richmond,
where her husband's love was waiting,
and she died.

Oh, here is the sweet and polished blade of grace.
Here is the white knuckle of faith
against the grateful ache of memory.
And here is the sacramental hope:
Life is changed, not taken away.

Today birds circle through the mist
like beads for prayer,
a rosary of hope that the heart might hold.
And I see my cousin in their company,
some feathery motion against the rain,
some tender splash, like tears,
some possibility of permanence,
some shine.

WITHOUT
for Greg Blair

When death crashes through the heart house
we had hoped would keep us safe,
when death demands that we say its name,

when it rips the skin
from the bone of everlasting
and tears from us one
we have held and loved
and breathed as air we need,

when we are stunned and numbed
by a shapeless thing
we cannot hold or breathe,
we do not know
how to be or what to do
as we stumble toward our own
shaky salvation.

So we rage or we pray,
we weep or we sleep,
or we don't sleep,
at home
or not home.

We make arrangements.
We find a dress, or a tie,
we board a plane,
we gather as strangers to each other,
witnesses to ourselves,
seeking the secret of who we might be

as some way to remain here,
in this world,
without.

And we do what comes to us uncalled:
We wonder.
We edit, we revise, reconstruct.

A night, a morning, a moment,
a might-have-been-ordinary moment in May,
when the world wakes into bloom,
sings into life, and yet...

and yet Greg dies, he slips
into somewhere not here,
while we are left
on the other side of ordinary,
in the ever-after life
called *without,*

without a grammar for absence,
without a syntax for grief,
without a diagram
for the simple sentence,
Greg is dead.

For Greg has died without warning us
love me now,
love me here,
love me before I am gone.

Now we are here
without the long-ago child,
without the long-haired boy,
without the unsettled teen
in the unsettling haze of escape,
without the glory-graced man
we had held before sunlight went dark.

And we have only this,
our own desperate voice
clamoring through the heart house
until it stalls at the door called kindness,
until it slides through that door, and stills,
until it chooses what it wants to remember.

We are the living.
We can choose.
We can insist that memory has a name
spelled in four letters called Greg,
a name sung out loud
by a choir of letters called love.

VI

You are looking through the grace of what goes on,
to what you keep, even when you let go.

Witness

I watched today from high above the sea
as three swans circled near the fishing rocks,
then disappeared, as though I'd made them up,
as though they somehow could not be as real
as icy pines or frozen steps that led
from where I stood to where they swam.

I blinked, no more than that, and they were there.
I blinked again, and nothing. They were gone.

Perhaps it never happened quite this way.
No one was there to say. But I believe
there has to be a symmetry of grace
in such a gift as late December swans
in easy glide, three willing things
content to be exactly what they are:

Three lives in equal harmony and trust
at Christmas, in this place, in this sweet while.

GLOW

You glow like someone in love, the stranger said,
and yes, I said, trying to tell how living
at the beach was love in blush and bloom,
how it was patience, the tide rising and falling
without me, roses blossoming on the bluff
when they were ready,

all my will that they flower Now! or Now! useless
as willing the sand be stone free for summer feet.
Mornings, I would watch the sun lift from the sea
like a reluctant finger of light,
like a lover who could not bear
to let go the body that had held him close.

Stay? Leave?
Everywhere, the questions are the same.

For a long while, I did not think
that I could leave the beach or the land
where I had lived in quiet bliss.
Then came an answer called cancer,
the darkness that batters the brain
and shuns the light of seasoned love.

Welcome the new, said Rilke,
full of things that have never been.

So I came to Colorado,
land of clinics and dreamable cures,
and here I live a different joy,
the grace of grandchildren falling toward me

and mountains rising above,
as old love makes room for new love

in the snowglow of being alive.

Morning, Miller Place

The pond has not been frozen much this year.
The mallards look content. It must be grand
to waddle near the water free from fear
of winter boys with pucks and sticks in hand.

Beyond the pond the road curves toward the beach.
I follow, and I laugh at how the sun
can tempt me to believe that spring's in reach
and tease me into leaving work undone.

Down at the Sound, seduced by gentle air,
by sea and sand and endless blue above,
I open and surrender darker care
to morning's touch, its light and easy love.

It folds along my bones like second skin.
It floats around my heart, then settles in.

HERE AND THERE, SEPTEMBER

The sun so strong today the pink impatiens
shrivel to themselves and turn away.
Even the hose, too hot to stay hard,
looks limp and lazy, lost without relief.
You know how it goes, your heart shrinking
while it learns to live its half-life, left alone.

I have not walked through where you are in autumn,
I have not felt September splash my skin to cooling
while it dares the world around to blaze toward dying
beauty, bold, so brief it can't abuse.

But in the tracks you make today,
the shape of me lies twisted into you,
dirt, grass, ivy path, and leaves.
I'm in your upstate smell of summer gone,
in wind that sweeps the stale, damp sway of August
and sings to you new season, time
we move.

And here downstate, in the holly-
berry promise of October born
inside hot day, you are
holding, still.

In Corte Madera
for Sergio Baroni

Come to Corte Madera,
where you will find the man
who will sit with you
in shadow or light,
who will wander with you
through the airless hall
toward the open window,
who will lead you to the door
that locks in the day

when your daughter took
the scissors to her skin,

when you twisted the letter of *love*
until it was *lone*, then *alone*,

when you forgot that home is where
they're supposed to take you in.

Come find the man
who will work with you
to loosen the lock,
to unclose the door,
and for a radiant while
you will become the joy
you have been afraid of
for too long.

Come to Corte Madera.
You will find light
streaming everywhere,
from you.

Leaving Middlebury

for Danny Ackerman

Maybe it was the mountains, the way
you knew that they would hold
you to them, close, like a mother deep
in love with the child she names her own,
how they were green and new
to you, even as they had long

stood sky-bound, however such things can long
and reach to heaven, a way
to grow. You came here new
from home, from the place that would hold
the early naming of things you would own
like your breath, like your heartbeat, trails and
    woods deep

with discovery, trees so leafy tall, holes so deep
that you would never need to know that long
and high and wide would not always be your own
as you pushed your way
through and over what would never hold
you down. Stars, too, and moon, new

through your window each night, you watched
    and knew
their movement, the startling, bone-deep
hint of what would hold
you, carry you along
like current to drift your way
inside your heart, a secret space you'd always name
    your own.

And the early waves, to own
their swell and crash, your body new-
muscled and brown with sun, you found a way
to trust yourself to what beats deep
under skin, a primal longing
rhythm, a move and sway and hold

on you in pulsing promise that life will not withhold.
So you came to these mountains to own
some momentary path of play and trick, some longer
staying light, forever curving up and down, the shape of
    you new
carved in snow and dirt, in tracks deep
with whispers that you had passed this way.

And so the going, easier now, you own a deepened
sense of woods and sky, of new known truths and faith
    from long
ago, of ways to lift and rise, of how to hold.

ORIENTEERING

You hold the compass close until you find
direction that reveals what we must know:
that sometimes we must learn to fall behind
before we understand how we can go.

We listen to the space between the trees
where quiet cold and snow have settled light.
It tells us faith's the bridge that helps to ease
the aching disconnectedness we fight.

So we surrender here to sky and air,
let go of hurts and fears we've long embraced,
and in complete communion, truest prayer,
allow these woods to grant us healing grace.

Alone, we find the reverence to believe.
Together, we discover how to leave.

COMMENCEMENT

You came cold, frozen
in the February landscape,
wondered at this woman
wanting gifts you had not given:
the gift of self inside your winter self.

Closed, like seed in hard soil,
your longing was light,
heat thick with healing,
the gray-gone-green of springtime
singing itself to life.

And she, needing the knowing of you,
needing, finally, her own knowing,
watched you thaw, melt into April,
flower from inside.

Today she gathers the beauty of you,
green and growing
and hopeful to her heart.
She breathes your blooming.

LAST CLASS

One day it happens,
you notice green stalks
spring through winter ground,
hear their scattered play as
some wild summons,
some insistent call
to what is pushing through you,
and you make it into metaphor

for your own abandon,
your own spinning exit
to what comes next.
Then it's June, come
with its own calendar,
its way of closing down on days
wide with heat and sky,
its own kind of reckoning.

It's June, another last day, one
like thirty others, until the boy
who refuses you easy release
speaks the simple syntax you have
lent them, the declarative sentence
that belongs to these
forty minutes of afternoon:
It's your last class.

In the freeze-frame of silence
that follows, that comes cold
and quick like fog against skin,
you watch them hold
to the haze of still breath,
to the white pulse of waiting,

and you tell them
the clearest word you own,

the word you heard when March
muscled through brown earth,
moved through you,
and you answered *yes,*
that little sigh of syllable,
that link of longing and loss.
And because you are finally
out of images, out of time,

because a bell will soon
sing that it is summer
and they will spill
to the hill beyond,
you look at them like
some first flower,
some winged thing that
will not fly by again.

You are looking through
the grace of what goes on,
to what you keep,
even when you let go.

ABOUT THE AUTHOR

Maureen Sweeney Ackerman, a lifelong writer, reader, and runner, and recipient of multiple awards for excellence in teaching, has taught creative writing to high school students and facilitated poetry and memoir workshops for adults. "Poetry is my heartbeat," she says. "It's how I grieve, how I celebrate, how I see and hear and process the world." Until 2017, she lived on Long Island, where running along the beach gave rise to many of her poems. She currently lives in Denver, Colorado.

Photo by Jeff Shusterman

Made in the USA
San Bernardino,
CA